Praise for *Sync*

Sync or Swim is a quick and easy read with a simple but powerful message for anyone who hopes to effectively manage and lead others. It reminds us of what we all need to remember but too quickly forget—that everyone needs appreciation, but that everyone needs it communicated in their own unique way. This book is a beautiful introduction to the basics of the true art of appreciation in the workplace.

—JACK CANFIELD | Coauthor of *The Success Principles* and *Chicken Soup for the Soul at Work*

I've always said that business is easy . . . until people get involved. The key word is teamwork. If you can't work together, you can't win together. In *Sync or Swim*, Chapman, White, and Myra tell a quick, fun story that gives you the tools you need to bring your people together like never before.

—DAVE RAMSEY | *New York Times* bestselling author and nationally syndicated radio show host

I was sitting waiting to board a flight, with twenty things on my to-do list. But I decided to look at this fable . . . and couldn't stop reading! It really drew me in and I instantly started thinking about how I need to purposefully tell (and show) my amazing team members how much I genuinely appreciate them—and to do so much more often. *Sync or Swim* makes a tremendously important point in an incredibly simple way—that I don't think I'll ever be able to forget.

—SHAUNTI FELDHAHN | Author, *For Women Only* and *The Male Factor*

Congratulations! *Sync or Swim* is a quick and easy read with valuable insights. Wherever you work, whatever your role, you will see yourself and your team in this little story . . . and you will learn. Extremely well done.

—GARY BRADT, PHD | Primary trainer for *Who Moved My Cheese?* Author, *The Ring in the Rubble: Dig Through Change and Find Your Next Golden Opportunity*

Not since Patrick Lencioni's *The Five Dysfunctions of a Team* has someone encapsulated a critical leadership lesson in a quick and fun-to-read fable. After fifteen years as a turnaround executive and seven years as a leadership coach, I recognized old familiar patterns in *Sync or Swim* and picked up several new useful techniques for keeping executive teams motivated and working together. A valuable and enjoyable read!

—GLENN HELLMAN | CEO, DrivenForward; executive coach

In an age fixated on quarterly results, bottom-line growth, and increased value for the stakeholders, this book turns our attention to HOW those results get produced. The people who make them happen (or not) are real-life human beings, not cogs in a machine. And each of them is unique. *Sync or Swim* sheds valuable light on the everyday human interactions that can make or break any organization. Leaders and managers will do well to take heed.

—DEAN MERRILL | Publishing executive and bestselling author/collaborator of more than forty titles

"It's about people, stupid." That's the first line in our book *Brains on Fire* and that's the big management lesson I learned reading *Sync or Swim*. We all want to be seen as individuals. And heard. This short fable is a simple and wonderful reminder.

—ROBBIN PHILLIPS | Courageous President, Brains on Fire
Coauthor, *Brains on Fire* and *The Passion Conversation*

Sync or Swim points out how easy it can be to help others improve their performance with positive affirmation, genuine encouragement, and open communication. Every manager and executive will recognize themselves—and others—in this fun, readable tale.

—JUDY BRYSON | Pioneer Clubs president/CEO, retired

There are many Friscos, Tias, Alanas, et al in the workplace. The trick is for managers to appreciate the differences and lead accordingly. This book will help managers appreciate people for WHO they are and recognize them for what they DO in an appropriate manner.

—PETER W. HART | CEO, Rideau Recognition, Inc.

I was surprised at how I was drawn into *Sync or Swim*, despite the fact that I'm a lover of practical, proven management case studies. This fresh and creative approach gave me insights on how to appreciate, understand, and communicate with each colleague through their eyes that I wouldn't have gotten from any "typical" business book. Now I'm challenged to put into practice these unforgettably practical lessons.

—JOHN LaRUE | Founder, ChristianityToday.com
Chief Development Officer, Jesus.net

The title *Sync or Swim* was not lost on me. As a leader, I not only see myself and my team in Chapman, White, and Myra's latest book, I identify things we could have done much better in our own journey. If you lead or ever want to lead, this is a must-read. You did it again guys!

—MIKE NOVAK | President and CEO, KLOVE

I really enjoyed the story and the perspective it gives business leaders at all levels. *Sync or Swim* is a great, easy read with a terrific message that allows the reader see the value of targeted, sincere appreciation.

—MIKE BYAM | Terryberry Company

Sync or Swim is a compelling tool for management training and a refresher course for those who've spent years leading people. You'll find yourself smiling and resonating with the sequence of events in this delightful fable.

—CAROL THOMPSON | Chief Operating Officer, Christianity Today

Sync or Swim is a brilliant modern-day fable that captures the essence of everything that is wrong in the workplace, and it offers real, authentic solutions steeped in practical wisdom! If you manage people or plan to in the future, you must read this fable!

—AARON BROYLES | Entrepreneur, speaker, and author of *Do Great Things*

Sync or Swim

A FABLE ABOUT IMPROVING WORKPLACE CULTURE AND COMMUNICATION

Gary Chapman, Paul White, and Harold Myra

NORTHFIELD PUBLISHING · CHICAGO

Edited by Betsey Newenhuyse
Interior and cover design: Erik M. Peterson
Cover and interior illustrations copyright © 2014 by
Nathan Little/nathanlittleart.com. All rights reserved.
Gary Chapman photo: P.S. Photography
Paul White photo: Michael Bankston

Library of Congress Cataloging-in-Publication Data

Chapman, Gary D.
  Sync or swim : a fable about workplace communication and coming
together in a crisis / Gary Chapman, Paul White, Harold Myra.
    pages cm
  ISBN 978-0-8024-1223-2 (hardback)
  1. Employee motivation. 2. Employee morale. 3. Communication
in management. 4. Organizational behavior. 5. Corporate culture.
I. White, Paul E. II. Myra, Harold Lawrence. III. Title.

HF5549.5.M63C4383 2014
  658.4'5—dc23
                        2014029144

          ISBN: 978-0-8024-2216-3

We hope you enjoy this book from Northfield Publishing. Our goal is to provide high-quality, thought-provoking books and products that connect truth to your real needs and challenges. For more information on other books and products that will help you with all your important relationships, go to www .moodypublishers.com or write to:

Northfield Publishing
820 N. LaSalle Boulevard
Chicago, IL 60610

1 3 5 7 9 10 8 6 4 2

Printed in the United States of America

*To all those determined to help their teams
pull together when the storms hit*

Contents

Why We Wrote
Sync or Swim

Perhaps you've noticed something in your workplace, something pollsters are reporting as sobering contradictions. Up to 90 percent of American organizations have a recognition program, yet the majority of workers say they receive no recognition. The number-one reason Americans leave their jobs is because they don't feel appreciated. Then there's this: over half of all managers think they do a good job of recognizing employees, but only 17 percent of workers agree that's true of their managers.

Those are hard realities, considering most workers (67%) say they're more motivated by praise from managers than anything else—including money.

Workplaces have become high-pressure environments demanding more production with fewer resources. Employees worry about the economy and their future, and they often feel used and undervalued. One of the most disturbing trends we've tracked is the sharp increase of cynicism.

"They don't give a rip about me," one worker told us, "only my performance."

We've also noticed something that's more hopeful—a great thirst for solutions. Since negative trends have spread in businesses, healthcare, government agencies, and non-profits, the bright ray of hope is that everyone is looking for ways to make things better.

Through our work with thousands of employees we've discovered practical principles for making recognition and appreciation authentic. We've trained leaders to use those principles to help their organizations thrive and become healthy, positive places to work.

And we've written a fable that illustrates those practical principles.

Why? Since earliest times, fables have been passed on from generation to generation. As scholars attest, humans are "hard-wired for story." Fables cut through complexity to reveal simple wisdom. In them we see our own predicaments and reactions, both wise and foolish.

Sync or Swim helps us solve the frustrating contradiction of morale-building programs hurting morale and of "recognition" resulting in cynicism. The story is written to be a fun, quick read, illustrating ways to communicate authentic appreciation that generates productivity and effective teamwork. The bear, squirrel, bird, beaver, chipmunk, and cat all respond in different ways—as each of us as individuals does.

We shared *Sync or Swim* with a wide variety of managers, trainers, and other leaders, and among the many responses were these:

- "Because of my heavy workload and new demands, I identified with the characters' pain. In my second reading I found myself getting drawn in and enjoying it even more. I love the realism and practical insights!"
- "We've all struggled with these issues, and the principles are so wonderfully illustrated. The story is an easy read for everyone, including those who don't read very much."
- "The fable is a great tool for groups to create awareness, stimulate lively discussion, and give hope for changing their current atmosphere into a thriving workplace."

Another respondent sent us this reaction: "The characters are so true to what we're like—we're often oblivious in just the ways they are!"

After the fable you'll find more of their responses to stimulate your thinking. But first, we invite you to read *Sync or Swim*.

GARY CHAPMAN

PAUL WHITE

HAROLD MYRA

Sam Comes to Paradise

Sam the Shetland sheepdog loved big challenges, and landing his dream job as CEO of Monarch Enterprises, the family-run company that owned Spruce Isle, felt like the challenge of a lifetime. Standing atop the island's seawall, he studied the breach where storm waters had blasted through a while back, flooding several streets and shops and impacting Monarch's bottom line. His mandate was to ensure it never happened again and that Spruce Isle's all-important tourist trade would continue to grow and flourish.

Friends had warned him that it wouldn't be easy, and that as CEO he'd be caught between Monarch's head-in-the-sand board and its prickly staff. Sam sniffed the sea air. He had years of experience dealing with prickly personalities. *I'll get them on board and get it done!*

The sun was bright, the breezes warm, and it was hard to imagine the fury of a storm assaulting the levees. Tourists

Bring on the storms!

were filing off the ferry at the dock and heading for the quaint shops and restaurants renowned for their seafood. The ocean's blues, greens, and frothy whites lifted his spirits.

All his life Sam had dreamed of coming here. Spruce Isle was named for its majestic trees on the mountains and famed for its flowers and butterflies, including a species that swarmed in its forest each year. Everything—shops, mountains, butterfly migrations, beaches, and even the system of storm barriers—everything invigorated him.

Bring on the storms! His resolve rippled through him like a shot of adrenaline.

Looking out at smaller, distant islands, he noticed a seabird flying toward him. As it neared, he saw it was a puffin. It soared in, landed, settled itself, and stared out at the sea.

Sam had seen puffins in photos. He thought of them as odd but somehow natty seabirds, with their white faces and black caps and stout, multicolored beaks. But this one looked tattered, her chunky body a bit unsteady on her red-orange feet.

The old puffin said, "Bigger storms are coming." She hunched forward as in a stiff wind.

Sam glanced her way. She'd be amazed, he thought, to know he was in charge of leading the entire Monarch organization and protecting the island. He had come from the turbulent world of sports management with a reputation as a problem solver, someone who could work with big egos. Whatever it took, he'd rally the team and get it done.

The puffin flapped her stubby wings and shifted her weight. "The next storm could bring disaster."

Sam looked over at her. *I know that. What's with this bird?*

The puffin wagged her head, eyes still on the sea. Then her short wings suddenly beat furiously, lifting her into the air.

Annoyed and slightly unsettled, Sam watched until she became a little speck in the distance.

"We're understaffed and underfunded."

The Bear on
the Mountain

Sam started climbing the mountain that dominated the island's interior. Its wildlife, trails, and butterfly pavilion drew thousands of tourists, and they were drawing him. Eventually he was looking down on the shoreline below, a long, thin squiggle of brown separating the ocean blue and island green. That squiggle had to hold back the coming storms from the lowland shops, beach, and hotel.

He reached the highland forest with tall oaks and pines and meadows bright with wildflowers. Although early for the swarming butterflies the island was famous for, blue swallowtails circled a puddle and orange-tips zigzagged over a meadow. A bird chirped and a feathery flash of scarlet caught his eye.

Sam passed hikers studying a trail marker and went on to the butterfly pavilion, one of the island's most popular attractions. After standing in line with other visitors and then entering the vaulted enclosure, he feasted his eyes on the hundreds of butterflies on the trees and plants and in the air. A poster on the wall helped him identify clear-wings, swordtails, cabbage whites, and painted ladies. He watched light play on sparkling metallic colors of a metal-mark. A hovering leafwing landed on his shoulder and stayed there a while.

The experience was all he'd hoped.

Yet the pavilion itself was in need of paint and a bit shabby, with cobwebs in corners. He'd take that up with Frisco, the head ranger.

Sam followed a trail to the preserve's headquarters, a complex of log buildings with flags flying, including Monarch's corporate flag—sky-blue, with a monarch butterfly poised on the leaf of a gnarly branch.

Monarch's proud history started with a pioneer who saw the island's potential for tourism despite the danger-ous storms. Over time the company built seawalls, devel-oped hotels and shops, and cut trails so visitors could see the butterflies swarm. Much of the forest was set aside for camping and hiking. Then came the butterfly pavilion, and tourism spiked.

Sam found Frisco in his headquarters cabin. The big spectacled bear stared at him. "Heard you were coming." His expression said he'd like to send Sam back out the door with a swipe of his paw.

Sam's hair bristled but he forced out friendly words of wonder at the butterfly pavilion. He said nothing about its cobwebs but quizzed Frisco on his priorities.

The ranger's responses confirmed what Sam had heard: Monarch workers were very good at playing the blame game. "We're supposed to have emergency shelters up here all stocked and ready in case a storm breaches the levees," Frisco blustered. "But go look for yourself. They're not ready because we requisition supplies but the stuff never arrives!"

Sam perked up his ears. "I'll check on that."

"We're understaffed and underfunded. Hordes of tourists keep coming, and we can't worry about shelters we'll never need." The big bear reared up higher and stared down at his new boss. His meaning was clear: The seawall is your problem, and you don't look like you can handle it.

Sam had dealt with plenty of big pro athletes. He stared back.

Unblinking, Frisco complained, "My staff can't keep up with all these campers and gawkers. Headquarters *never* delivers on promises, and *nobody* cares." He thrust a list at Sam. "Here's what we need."

Sam took the list. He wondered what the rest of his direct reports would be like.

"You wouldn't believe all the negativism around here!"

Tia's Complaints

That night Monarch's senior staff welcomed Sam with dinner in a restaurant overlooking the harbor—but Sam didn't feel welcome at all. During his short speech, no one smiled at his attempts at humor. Frisco yawned, and others looked down at their phones. Sam knew they all felt underpaid and underappreciated by Monarch, and they resented having no say in the CEO selection. Sam was their third new leader in two years.

Next morning he arrived early at the office and saw Tia, the plump gray squirrel who headed human resources, was already at her desk. As he worked studying charts showing needed seawall repairs, he noticed employees going in and out of her office. Mid-morning, when she was finally alone, he stepped across the hall and asked sympathetically, "Long, busy morning?"

Tia looked up from organized stacks. "Longer than you know." She thrust the short stack toward him. "I've been compiling these reports for you."

As he glanced at them, she made a sharp clicking sound. "You won't like what you read."

"Why?"

"You'll see." The white tips of her bushy tail swished defensively. "Start with the exit interviews."

Tia's downcast look made Sam try to encourage her. "Employees leave for all kinds of reasons. Exit interviews are always full of complaints."

She shrugged. "Too many are leaving."

"Any sense of why?"

"Yes! Over and over they say nobody cares about them, only that they get their work done." Tia's intensity was softened with motherly concern. "They're skilled employees! They're good people, and we're losing too many."

Sam promised to study the reports.

What he read made Tia's point starkly clear. An engineer complained, "I'm expected to do more with less, yet faster and better. But I'm working flat-out."

A data-entry worker said, "Nobody cares about me. I'm invisible . . . except when I make a mistake. Then, watch out!"

An accountant explained why he quit: "I felt used—and never supported."

The reports described turf wars and endless red tape, deadlines missed, and conflicts and mistrust among supervisors. No departments were rated as having "high morale."

Sam put down the reports. He didn't find them discouraging—in fact, just the opposite. They energized him, the way years before seeing a puppy drowning in a lake had spurred him to race to its rescue.

Late afternoon he visited Tia's office and affirmed he was taking the reports seriously.

"I hope so. Frankly, you may be in over your head."

Sam waited for more.

Tia's tail twitched impatiently, and then she confessed she felt like climbing the walls. "You wouldn't believe all the negativism around here!" She made a sound like a stifled sneeze and then shook her head. "How am I supposed to help employees when they won't work together, and they sit around blaming each other for all the lost work orders and not meeting deadlines?"

Sam Throws a Party

Through his office window, Sam watched tourists entering shops and restaurants and heading for the beach. Vacationing families and hikers, birders, photographers, and butterfly enthusiasts had no idea the barriers were in poor repair.

A squall had swept in overnight, reminding him the storm season was upon them. He had barely slept, thinking about the dysfunctional teams, weakened levees, and the catastrophe that could happen on his watch.

He had to turn this organization around—and fast! He had handled big-ego players and agents. He relished building team spirit, he knew he was good at it, and he was ready to get moving.

Monarch, he learned, put a lot of money into tourist promotional events but did nothing for employee morale. He decided to change that in a big way and started working with team leaders to create a splashy, inspiring "celebration."

He would emphasize the heroics of Monarch's pioneers. He commissioned graphics for the big screen to show breached-levee devastation. He asked Tia to work with supervisors to identify employees deserving awards.

The Monarch Celebration Luncheon was held in a hotel ballroom and included music, banners, good food, skits, and a funny guest emcee. Then Sam took the microphone while huge, graphic images of storm surges flooding the island's shops and hotels appeared on a screen. He was brutally honest about the weaknesses of the seawall, and then he shifted to his we-can-do-it speech. "In the spirit of our island's visionary pioneers, we can strengthen those seawalls, and we can make this world-class attraction better than ever."

Sam was the coach in the locker room inspiring his team. He was the storyteller showing how working together was the way to exceed expectations.

Supervisors then presented awards to selected employees, and Sam presented special ones, including a significant award to Tia for her constant work on behalf of her fellow employees.

That night Sam finally got a full night's sleep.

"You sure you want to hear all this?"

Briana Tells
the Truth

Next morning he wandered over to Tia's office, hoping to bask in the afterglow of the celebration. Instead, he found her dispirited.

He remembered right after the program she'd disappeared, and this morning she had shown up late. He asked, "You feeling okay?"

"I'm all right." She averted her eyes and turned back to her work.

Sam stood there for a moment, wondering. *Now what?*

Briana sat in a nearby cubicle. A bright young chipmunk, she was a college intern on board for the tourist season. Sam pegged her as a go-getter. She was quick and observant, alert to everything going on. He decided she'd be perfect to sniff out what was happening.

"Briana, are you up for a field trip?"

"Of course!" she responded quickly. "What do you need me to do?"

"I want you to visit every department, repair team, and the forest preserve staff. Talk to them. Make notes. See how they're feeling about things."

After two days she returned to Sam's office. Without hesitation she reported she'd been blown away by the widespread cynicism.

Briana was no-nonsense and feisty. She told him flat-out his morale-building luncheon may have done more harm than good. Most considered it a waste of their time, calling it "a stupid pep rally," and those who got awards felt they were phony.

"Is that what Tia thought?"

"Not exactly. She's fed up with everything, and she gets embarrassed in front of a crowd—especially when there's so much sarcasm about the awards."

They're sarcastic about my giving them awards?

"You sure you want to hear all this?" the young intern asked.

He nodded yes, but he really wanted to plug his ears.

"Employees view you as the 'Mighty Motivator' trying to manipulate them—and they have nicknames for you I won't repeat. I hate to say it, but they mock you as a 'young pup' promoted above your skills level."

Briana said all this as if she were describing an interesting movie, simply trying to capture the plot and characters. "I noticed something else," she added. "The flood part of your speech got through. There's a lot of finger-pointing, and a lot of anxiety about what will happen if a really big storm hits."

"I've heard about your troubles. I see it all the time."

Seawall Wisdom

Sam was devastated. He walked the streets looking in shop windows, and he ate lunch alone in a small bistro. Tourists around him were all having a good time, and he envied them. Maybe, he thought, if he climbed up on the seawall as he had his first day on Spruce Isle, he could gain perspective.

His tail drooped behind him as he climbed. On the parapet looking out at the ocean, he asked himself what was going on. He had paid his dues. He was no "young pup." He'd done his best to lift their spirits, but all these workers did was bicker and pass the buck. He fantasized about quitting and working in the little bistro, or going up in the mountains to live in a simple cabin where—flood or no flood—he'd be dry and safe. He was baffled.

A smudge in the distance slowly became a puffin flying toward him.

As it came closer, Sam wondered if it was the same one

he'd seen his first day. When he'd described that puffin to Tia, she'd reacted with excitement, thinking it might have been Olympia. She was a legend on the island as a successful entrepreneur, distinguished professor, and consultant to major corporations. Tour guides always mentioned that Olympia lived on Spruce Isle.

The puffin soared in, landed, and settled herself the same place as before.

Tia had told Sam he'd know it was Olympia by an identifying mark on her black cap. And there it was: an irregular white splotch.

The old puffin said nothing. Sea breezes gusted over them.

They watched a ship dock and tourists descend the gangplank. A family of terriers, the instant they were off, barked joyfully and chased one another up a hill. Guitar music from the outdoor cafes floated up. Visitors were blissfully unaware of what a big storm might do to them.

Olympia turned toward Sam. "I've heard about your trouble. I see it all the time."

"What?"

"Toxic work cultures."

Sam wrinkled his nose. "No place could be as toxic as Monarch!"

"You'd be surprised."

Olympia spoke with authority, yet with kind concern. She told him she'd heard about employees mocking his awards program.

He winced. "You wouldn't believe their sarcastic comments!"

She nodded sympathetically. "Sarcasm is poison. It kills morale." Then she added, "Monarch's employees have suffered a long time. Changing the culture will take a whole new way of communicating."

He bristled. *How about the way they communicate about me?*

"Ever run a machine without oil?" she asked. "Pretty soon, metal grinds against metal. Without it, worker grinds on worker. Sparks ignite resentments and then cynicism. What's vital is communicating *authentic* appreciation. It's organizational oil."

"But that's just what I was doing! They received awards for what their supervisors said they did right."

She gave him another sympathetic look. "So what do you think you did wrong?"

Sam flared. "I don't think I did anything wrong!"

Olympia told him to relax and take a long step back. "When workers feel used and not valued as individuals, rewarding them for what they've done backfires. They have to feel valued for more than just what they can produce. They're persons, not replaceable parts."

That made Sam flare even more. "I never treated them that way!"

"I'm sure you didn't," she responded smoothly. "Yet

they called your program a pep rally. Morale-building events must make sense in a culture of appreciation, or else they come off contrived." She paused. "What most managers don't understand is, you can't communicate genuine appreciation with a broad brush."

Sam tried not to be defensive. Yet as she went on and on about authentic appreciation, he kept thinking, *Yes, but leadership requires action and accountability.* He finally said bluntly, "Communicating appreciation is fine, but it's no magic bullet."

Olympia stared at him. Then, for the first time she spoke sharply. "Sam, everyone needs to feel valued. Work is tough and full of harsh realities. Authentic appreciation isn't a magic bullet, but the magic dies when it's missing!"

They were both silent for a time.

When she spoke again, she had softened. "You described Tia's embarrassment about getting on stage to receive her awards. She's the perfect example of what I'm talking about. She's a real gem. Yet you have to communicate with her as a unique individual. As the old saying goes, 'Different strokes for different folks.'"

Sam doubted that fit. "How could anyone not like getting praised?"

The wise old puffin smiled. "There's your blind spot! Why doesn't everyone love public praise? Because they're individuals! Because Tia is Tia. You're a sheepdog from a long line of sheepdogs who all loved being praised after doing a good job herding sheep. Like many leaders, you can't imagine others being different from you."

She stood and stretched her wings. "Here's tomorrow's assignment. Go listen to Tia. Pay attention to her signals."

Sam didn't know he had signed up for her assignments. He felt a twinge of resentment but admitted to himself that maybe she was on to something.

She lifted her wings to fly off, saying she'd see him tomorrow, same time, same place. "Sam, they've called you the Mighty Motivator, but what you have to learn is how to become the Great Listener."

As Olympia slowly became a small speck in the sky, he thought about that. She had said some really interesting things. He had taken to carrying a journal around to make notes in, and now he scrawled some of her insights:

Changing the culture requires
a whole new way of communicating.

What's vital is communicating authentic appreciation . . .
It's organizational oil.

When workers feel used and not valued,
rewarding them backfires.
They have to feel valued for more than what they produce.
They're persons, not replaceable parts.

Morale-building events must make sense
in a culture of appreciation, or they come off contrived.
Don't try to communicate appreciation with a broad brush.

Listening to Tia

B ack in the office, Briana was talking so fast her words seemed to be playing leapfrog. Half listening, Sam heard "weak seawalls and storms of the decade . . ."

"What did you say about 'storms of the decade'?"

"Native islanders are saying that's what's coming. They're all moving to higher ground."

Sam sighed. Maybe they were right. He had to get his teams repairing those levees! But how? Tia had the pulse of everything going on, and he asked Briana if she had arranged his lunch with her.

"Yes, a short one."

"Why short?"

"She seemed sorta frazzled."

Later he met Tia in the company cafeteria and they discussed agenda items. Then he leaned back and asked her to be totally candid. "It would help me to hear your honest assessment of the awards program."

Tia hesitated.

"Be *especially* candid if you think I don't want to hear it."

She smiled. "The program was premature. We weren't ready for it."

Tia confirmed diplomatically what Briana had told him brashly. He was tempted to ask why Tia hadn't warned him, but he knew he'd come as the new chief armed with his own ideas, determined to hit a home run. Instead, he had struck out.

Sam decided to ask the personal question. "I heard you were uncomfortable being brought up on stage."

This time she didn't hesitate. "Sure I was uncomfortable—but not because I was embarrassed about getting an award. I was worrying about what other employees were thinking."

Sam tried not to sound defensive. "Most people love to get awards."

"Sure, but did you know half of all employees are introverts?" She looked at him with a grin. "I'm shy, and I'm comfortable with that. We shy people get things done! In my job, I work to understand what individual employees are like and where they're coming from."

"What have you been learning about them?"

"They feel they're being used! They say no one listens to them."

Sam remembered Olympia emphasizing that not listening devalues workers, but listening and affirming empowers them. "What about you? Has anyone been listening to you?"

"No!"

She looked steadily at him, as if he shared the blame.

"Do you feel used?" he asked.

Tia dropped her eyes. "Lots of times."

Sam waited a long moment before he said, "I'll be listening."

Tia looked up. Then, in what he figured was her effort to be kind, she brightened and said his awards program hadn't failed completely. "You could see Alana loved it when you handed her that trophy."

Alana was the strikingly colorful bird who headed up sales and marketing. A scissortail flycatcher, she was warm, showy, and very smart.

Tia's tone had changed, and she winked. "Alana wouldn't be Alana if she didn't love awards. She knows how to give them and receive them, and she loves to strut her stuff. She keeps her enthusiasm, even when things are driving everybody else crazy."

Sam probed for more insights on key employees. Then he asked what Tia most enjoyed about her job, and after that how she was surviving the frustrations of this busiest season. He made no pronouncements or suggestions. He kept listening, trying to put himself in her place.

Then he asked the question that made her tear up. "What concerns you the most right now?"

Instantly she said, "The deadline for compliance! Those new government regulations have to be implemented two weeks from today." She described how vague and confusing the regs were and how stiff the noncompliance penalties.

Tia at that moment looked frazzled indeed.

"I've got to do this right," she explained, "but the small print is endless, and everyone in the industry is confused. If I get this wrong, and if you have to bring in the pricey lawyers and pay the fines, all my work won't count for anything. It's my responsibility, but I'm not sure *anybody* can get this done right."

Glimmers of Hope

"You were speaking Tia's language," Olympia said. They were atop the seawall again, and Sam had just described his coming alongside Tia to cope with those anxiety-arousing regulations. All afternoon he had studied them, and then he'd had dinner with her and a consultant to hash out the ambiguities. In the morning, he'd helped her set a course of action.

As he shared this with Olympia, Sam had come alive, his tail curled high. "When we finally got the wording nailed, Tia had a whole new spirit."

"You helped her free the key log in her logjam."

"It took time and effort, but it changed the chemistry between us."

Olympia nodded. "Sometimes all it takes is helping someone with a task. That's what some employees most appreciate."

Whoa! Sam felt a stab of caution. "I don't have time or

skills to give hands-on help to everybody."

With a touch of amusement Olympia said, "Not everybody wants your help! Some will welcome it as Tia did, but others will resent it as meddling. You have to pick up individual signals."

"Most of the signals I'm getting say, 'I don't trust you.'"

Olympia nodded again. "These teams have taken a long time to get this dysfunctional. You can't turn it around in a day—but you can get started. Keep your messages sweet and simple, in languages they understand, with actions they value. Tone of voice and body language often say more than words."

Sam got that, but he didn't want to waste time holding people's hands. He felt internal alarms going off. While he was doing all that touchy/feely stuff, the storms could strike!

A blue-and-white swallowtail sailed past, arced out over the ocean, and then returned to alight beside a tiny puddle. It seemed content to simply float on breezes and drink nectar in the sunshine. Sam still had moments when he longed to escape to one of those cabins in the mountains, far above floods and sarcasm.

Olympia was saying, "If you're going to lead, know your followers."

"I just got here, so I don't know much."

"I'm glad you realize that! Tell me what you *do* know about each of your direct reports."

After he had described his impressions, she advised, "Remember, they all like appreciation for doing a good job, but they also want to be valued for who they are—not just what they produce." She paused for emphasis. "Communicating authentic appreciation isn't simplistic, like checking off a checklist."

Sam cocked his head with an I-don't-get-it look.

"Workers are like characters in a really good novel. They have a wide range of personalities and motivations. It takes genuine, personal appreciation to bring out their greatest capacities."

He frowned. "So you have to be a psychologist?"

"Sam, you're smart. It's not all that difficult. You can learn how to do it."

After she flew off, he pulled out his journal and added a few things he wanted to remember.

KEEP YOUR MESSAGES SWEET AND SIMPLE, IN LANGUAGES THEY UNDERSTAND, WITH ACTIONS THEY VALUE.

TONE OF VOICE AND BODY LANGUAGE OFTEN SAY MORE THAN WORDS.

TEAM MEMBERS LIKE APPRECIATION FOR DOING A GOOD JOB, BUT THEY ALSO WANT TO BE VALUED FOR WHO THEY ARE—NOT JUST WHAT THEY PRODUCE.

"You corporate guys just don't get it!"

Jackson's Warning

Since Alana had received her award with enthusiasm, Sam felt like visiting her first. Yet he forced himself to start with Jackson. The big, smart beaver was an engineer, the guy charged with overseeing the completion of the long-neglected repairs.

Engineers intimidated Sam, but he had to get a sense of what was delaying everything.

Jackson showed up in his big vintage pickup truck, beautifully restored and painted cherry red. His hood ornament was a Monarch flag.

Sam had expected Jackson to be defensive about his unfinished work, but the beaver immediately played offense. "Climb aboard and see for yourself what's going on."

Jackson drove fast along the coast, flag flapping above his pickup's huge silver bumper. "You corporate guys just don't get it!" He shook his head and ground his teeth, big and white under his red hard hat. "Nobody cares. Nobody!

Where's the money we need for equipment? And where's the new staff to replace my guys who quit?"

Approaching a wide crack in the seawall, he abruptly hit his brakes. "Now, Sam, without equipment, supplies, and staff, how are we supposed to fix that gigantic crack? We've been requesting them for months!"

Jackson then hit the gas and drove on, pointing out more fissures. At a coastal curve, he yanked fast his emergency brake and leaned back in his seat. "You know the history, right?"

Sam did. Twenty years before, a massive storm had breached the conventional barriers. Sixteen persons had drowned. The outcry resulted in construction of state-of-the-art levees, with early warning systems.

"Everyone thinks it's all good as new," Jackson said, "but look at those old pilings pounded into the muck twenty years ago. They've deteriorated, and we need to replace them. Saltwater's seeping in everywhere. Doesn't anyone know we have a big storm coming?"

Jackson rammed the pickup in gear and drove on. As Sam listened to the experienced beaver, he was hearing a brew of bravado and frustration. And, he realized, fear.

"If these barriers are breached," Jackson said, "the storm will burst through and inundate everything. The hotels will be up to their eaves in surging waters, and wires in those waters could electrocute anyone touching one. Panic will spread. And ole Frisco up in the mountains won't be ready for all those evacuees."

"You'll have to light a fire under sweet old Henry."

The Money Game

Alana had the biggest office of all. Bigger than Sam's. Bigger than the conference room. After all, this was where celebrities were hosted.

Witty and flamboyant, Alana was a born entertainer. On her walls were photos of her hobnobbing with the famous singers, athletes, and other celebrities she would recruit for shows at the hotel. After she persuaded renowned naturalists to visit, the wonders of the isle began appearing in nature magazines. A large photo above her grand desk showed her up in the mountains flying a spectacular aerial stunt amidst swarming butterflies. That photo had graced a magazine cover with the caption "Bird of Paradise."

Alana had worked here forever, whereas Sam was just one of a long list of leaders who came and went. Unlike other employees, she was close to the family that owned Monarch. They loved her shows and the chance to meet the celebrities she brought to the island and, most of all, the way her efforts boosted their prosperity. When Alana greeted Sam with her melodic voice and invited him to relax on her brocaded couch, he felt like he was visiting royalty.

Good thing I met with Jackson first. We need much more money than the budget allows, and Alana could help us get it.

But first he listened to her tales of Monarch's legacy and her stories of all the celebrities who had accepted her invitations. She told him she had just talked to a rock star on a fifteen-city tour who assured her he was coming next week.

Sam listened as she described personal tidbits about bestselling authors and her triumphs of getting media coverage. He listened for a long time and concluded she was a genius of sales and persuasion.

Then he put the facts on the table: Monarch was far behind on payments to vendors, so they refused to fill orders for construction materials. Without them, repairs were stalled. Unless the board authorized the release of its hefty reserves, a big storm could break through.

Alana glanced at a large painting on her wall of Monarch's board members, all of them personal friends. With a knowing smile she said, "Why should they release more funds when operations just burns through its cash?"

He had heard about this—for years board and management had been locking horns over money. The board kept deciding the solution was to fire the leader and hire a new one. Well, Sam was not going to be their next victim.

"Alana," he said. "If they don't allocate the funds, a storm surge blasting through the levees could destroy this place."

She frowned. "I heard your speech, so you don't have to get dramatic on me. I could barely sleep after seeing your flood images on that big screen."

Sam insisted the next storm could make those images reality and that repairs had been delayed far too long. Alana responded the board was tired of hearing management crying wolf. She launched into stories about missed budgets and fired leaders.

As she talked, Sam remembered stories he'd heard about her—the way she procrastinated, missed details, and created messes her staff had to clean up.

Focus, Sam—now is not the time to think about that.

"Tell the board," Sam blurted out, interrupting her mid-story, "that if the levees fail, they'll experience unimaginable financial loss."

Alana went silent. Then her response surprised him. "*You* tell them," she declared, as if the matter was suddenly settled. "We'll go visit them together."

Elated, he told her that was exactly what he was about to propose.

Alana preened her feathers in a way that said the meeting was over. "I'll support your request, but you'll have to convince them you're running a tight ship. And you'll have to do your part. You'll have to light a fire under sweet old Henry."

Ah yes, old Henry.

From Alana's spacious office, Sam went directly to the cluttered corner long occupied by Henry, the old sea turtle who served as Monarch's comptroller. Henry was the one who needed to tighten budget controls, issue prompt financial reports, and stiffen sloppy collections procedures.

Close to retirement, Henry was looking forward to spending long, lazy hours meandering underwater. The old accountant loved details, hated change, and preferred things precise and orderly. He was a conformist, and right now he was conforming to the sour atmosphere around him. Sam listened patiently as he griped about younger employees' disregard for his procedures and how departmental bottlenecks were driving him crazy.

Alana was right. He had to light a fire under Henry.

He took him to lunch, and then he spent time with him exploring the quaint shops lining the streets. While craning his neck to see something on a low shelf, Henry's glasses nearly slipped off his face. He grumbled, "I'm always worrying my glasses will fall off and I'll smash them underfoot."

That sparked an idea. When they stopped in a drugstore, Sam found an eyeglass chain for him. Henry was delighted and affixed it to his glasses.

Sam spent the rest of the time learning about Henry. The old turtle was very responsive to his boss's questions about his career, painting heroic descriptions of times he had saved Monarch from financial disasters.

Sam kept brief his references to tardy reports and uncollected payments. From Henry's newly energetic responses, he sensed the old turtle would get started on the most urgent necessities.

The old accountant loved details, hated change,
and preferred things precise and orderly.

Brisk Winds and a Red Engine

A top the seawall, the puffin and the sheepdog watched a tourist ship bobbing and dipping in choppy waters. Brisk winds snapped the flags along the pier.

"They say something really big is coming," Sam said.

Olympia closed her eyes against the wind. "How are the repairs coming?"

"Jackson's waiting on supplies. Of course, in the meantime, he could do *something*. Jackson's as focused on fixing blame as fixing the levees." Sam described how he'd tried to express appreciation to Jackson, but the beaver would spin everything into a negative.

"I've had clients like that," she responded. "Complaining and blaming is so much easier than fixing problems."

Sam nodded. "But as I rode with Jackson, I got an idea. He's crazy about his truck, and he brags about what an incredible engine it has. So I got him a scaled, die-cast replica of it—cherry red." He smiled. "I had Briana wrap it,

Jackson opened it and loved it, and it's now hanging from his mirror."

Olympia nodded approval. "Sounds like you've pegged him right. Some value a gift more than anything you can say."

"I've been amazed at that. They're all so different! Alana loves recognition. Tia really responded to my jumping in to work with her, and Henry liked just hanging out and getting that little gift."

"And they're starting to see you as genuine—that you actually care about them and not manipulating them to get your jobs done."

"I hope so."

They watched the bobbing ship enter the harbor and ease into a dock. As winds buffeted the pier, deckhands helped the tourists navigate the gangplank. Sam said, "Right now I feel a lot like those visitors in the winds, barely keeping on their feet."

"You have a lot to handle right now."

Feeling at ease with Olympia, Sam admitted, "I dread confronting Giselle."

"Don't confront her! Timing is—"

"I know, I know. It's just that everyone tells me to watch out for her."

She greeted him with appraising eyes.

The Cat Who Spat

Through Monarch's lobby windows Sam watched Giselle, the silver Siamese chief of communications, on the beach with some of her staff. The elegant cat reigned over her teams of technicians and journalists from a home on the beach she had somehow managed to have the company purchase—a home with a storied history. It had belonged to a famed artist whose paintings of the isle's flowers and butterflies were always shown on the island promotions, along with a shot of the home with its curvy cedar-shake roof.

Sam's predecessor had warned him about her. "Giselle was a big reason I got fired," he told him. "She's brilliant, but she uses her brilliance to pollute staff morale with her double-edged comments. In her position she should be building morale, but she's always subtly putting the knife into management. She doesn't care one bit about the practical realities of running an organization, and she actually spat at me once."

The warning had sobered Sam. Up till now he'd mostly avoided her, but he realized he had to deal with the antagonism flowing from Monarch's communications center.

He decided to go first to Tia for her counsel.

On hearing he wanted her to assess Giselle, Tia's eyes tightened. As if treading treacherous ground, she carefully phrased a few suggestions. "Giselle has set opinions. Be careful."

Sam took a deep breath. "I've been told everyone fears her quick tongue. No one wants to cross her." He told her his predecessor had said she was aloof, caustic, and territorial.

Tia impatiently flicked her tail. "Don't paint her all one color! She's made some huge contributions here."

"Like?"

"She was the one with the vision to get the fashion industry to hold shows here. She helped Alana seal the deal. All those models on the runways and the international traffic to see them are because she had a vision, and she helped make it happen."

Sam's predecessor had explained that. Giselle had helped Alana pull off something very big and got something big out of it. She used her alliance with Alana to consolidate her power.

"I know Giselle is brilliant," Sam said. "But can she be trusted?"

"Maybe. She considers Monarch a tooth-and-claw environment. And she knows how to use her claws."

Sam stared at the storied home on the beach. He dreaded the walk to that house, fearing a battle with her could wreck everything. He studied his notes from Olympia, but none of them eased his fears about facing Giselle.

Having forced himself to walk over the sandy beach to her front door, he was surprised it was Giselle who opened it, as if she had been watching for him. She greeted him with appraising eyes, as if he were on one of her fashion runways.

She was in charge here.

For a long moment, neither spoke.

He had power. So did she.

He could fire her. She could retaliate.

If he fired her, she could incite rebellion in the ranks. Maybe he'd win . . . maybe she'd stand triumphant in the ashes.

Was this the way it was whenever Giselle met a new Monarch CEO?

Sam tried to sound friendly. As warmly as he could he said, "All my life I've seen pictures of this house. It's iconic."

"We've improved it over the years."

They engaged in small talk, after which she led him on a tour of the house, introducing employees at workstations that subtly blended into the home's décor. As they explored the gardens outside, he complimented her on her fashion industry coup, and he asked what on the island gave her the most satisfaction. Later, they sat on the deck and talked about her staff's skill sets and the pressures of producing so much content for so many publishing formats.

He felt on guard, as if he were countering her jabs. Yet with all their verbal fencing, he sensed over and over that she was someone who thought way out of the box. She sparked with ideas and when asked to unpack them, her command of detail was impressive. He told her that.

Eventually he raised the issue of how tragic it would be for the landmark home they were sitting in to be flooded and everything in it ruined. Giselle, curled up on a chaise, turned and looked directly at him, her blue eyes narrowed. "I've been thinking about that," she said. "And I have some ideas . . ."

The Wind Picks Up

O n his way to work, Sam noticed long swells riding in from far out to sea. A stiff wind was bending the scrub oak trees that dotted the island. Squally clouds streamed overhead.

It was coming.

Sam decided to check on Jackson's progress, and Briana begged to come as she had the day before.

"Why?"

"I want to become an engineer."

That surprised him. "When did you decide that?"

"Yesterday. In Jackson's truck, when he was telling us about the need for soft engineering and beach nourishment—new approaches to coastal protection."

Sam, impressed, said as they headed toward the work area, "You'd make a terrific engineer!"

For weeks he had been rushing from one manager to another, listening, communicating urgency and appreciation, and making sure money, communications, and supplies were flowing. They found Jackson hustling his workers as they drove in new pilings.

On seeing them, the engineer complained, "You can't just build seawalls and leave them without maintenance. This should have been fixed years ago. There's too much to do in too little time."

Sam nodded agreement. "I think it's coming soon."

"I know that!" Jackson pushed back his hard hat. "Three more days! We need three more days."

Briana said with her usual frankness, "The weather reports say you might not get them."

"Well then, lend a hand! Help us get this crack fixed." He recruited both of them to be gophers, fetching things for the workers. When the repair was completed, they watched Jackson rush off with his crew to the next crack in the seawall.

Storm!

Jackson got two days. Shop owners boarded up windows. Gale warnings were posted on the beaches—although as usual, curious tourists stood on the shore gazing at the churning waves. The ferries canceled their runs.

Suddenly the great horns sounded throughout the island. The sky darkened from slatey-gray to greenish-black and the trees bent sideways under blasts of winds from the sea. Sam and Briana were with Jackson at the seawall watching black clouds spreading to the horizon. Before long it seemed like night.

When the full energy of the storm hit they ran for the truck, and as they slammed the doors behind them, the rain pounded. Jackson gunned it through the downpour toward higher ground. As they lurched over ruts and rough ground, the little red engine replica dangling from the mirror bounced and swayed. Over the din of the hard rain Jackson shouted, "We're heading for a shelter I stocked!"

Sam couldn't see anything outside the truck and hoped Jackson could as he barreled on, teeth gritted beneath his hard hat. When they pulled up to the shelter, thunder boomed and a cluster of lightning lit up the wildness of the winds. "Can't make a dash for it now," Jackson warned.

Rain hammered on the roof and hood. Briana said, "That sounds like hail."

"It better not be!" Jackson exclaimed. "Not on my truck!"

The rain made a racket as winds whipped it against the truck in near-horizontal sheets. Lightning flashed again, and they saw a big tree crash, its roots splayed out.

They sat in the truck. It rocked from the force of the gales, and Jackson gripped the wheel as if to keep it upright. "These winds are ferocious! They'll cause a storm surge."

"Will the repairs hold?" Sam asked.

"How do I know? We had to do slapdash work, racing from one break to another! This storm could rip right through those repairs."

In the Shelter

The worst of the lightning finally eased up, though the rain continued to lash the truck. "Better make a run for it," Jackson said, opening his door. "Look out for downed power lines!"

Safe inside, Briana asked Jackson how worried he really was about the levees, and he launched into a brief lecture on structural integrity and the fact storm barriers are only as strong as their weakest points. The engineer liked answering Briana's questions because she was respectful, avidly interested— and scrappy the way he was.

In the shelter, they could hear the storm outside and settled in for the night. Sam asked Jackson about his family, and then Jackson asked Briana about hers. Sam told them both how much he appreciated all their efforts.

They talked until Jackson dozed off, but Briana stayed wired, listening for sounds of a storm surge bursting through. "One thing's sure," she said. "Whatever happens, we gave it our best shot."

He hadn't expected to hear that. He asked, "Despite my stupid pep rally?"

Briana replied that not everyone thought it was stupid. "Somehow afterwards we all started working as a team bit by bit. We kept getting it done and felt good about it. I really don't know just how all that happened."

You all started to feel listened to and valued. Sam pulled out his journal and started to share with Briana some of the things Olympia had taught him.

As they talked, the storm continued, and night came.

Sam wakened before dawn and realized the wind and rain had stopped. He stepped outside, into the dark. Drawing deep breaths in the moist, just-washed air, he wondered what dawn would reveal.

Slowly, rooftops became visible against sky. Purple storm clouds retreating to the east were streaked with red. He saw lots of trees down and debris blown against walls. Grabbing binoculars from Jackson's truck, he inspected the levees from his high vantage point.

All looked in order. No breaches, no flooding. The seawalls had held.

The Frisco Attitude

After two days of cleanup and thanking everyone who had helped in the crisis, Sam finally got up to the mountains to check on Frisco. Rangers were still clearing the trails of fallen trees.

Frisco was among them, chain saw in hand. He looked up at Sam's approach and commented on the storm's ferocity. Then he added with a slightly accusatory edge, "You missed the swarming."

Sam cocked his head.

"It's Spruce Isle's biggest event. It was over eight days ago."

Sam knew that. While he had been scrambling to get the dikes repaired, tourists were driving off to view the butterfly migration. Was Frisco miffed he hadn't shown up?

Frisco was saying, "I was right, wasn't I? About the seawalls holding. Once again, we didn't need the shelters."

Something inside Sam exploded. Didn't Frisco know

what it had taken to avert catastrophe? Didn't he get it that Sam and Jackson had saved him from being overwhelmed with flood refugees? He squelched the urge to tell him off.

Shoving down his anger, he asked how he could help with the cleanup on the trails. However, it soon became obvious Frisco didn't want his help. A falling beech tree had dragged down birch saplings, blocking a trail. Frisco clambered onto the big tree trunk and started making a strategic cut. Above the chain saw's roar he yelled, "You have to make sure it doesn't bind." He expertly topped the beech, nimbly jumping off at the right moment, then shook the birches loose.

"Well done," Sam said.

Frisco dismissed the compliment with a shrug that said his newbie boss knew nothing about how rough-and-ready guys got things done. He motioned for Sam to hop into his jeep, and they toured the storm damage and some glass breakage at the butterfly pavilion.

Sam spent several hours with him, but nothing he said or did thawed Frisco's gruff reserve.

But then, just as he was about to leave, rangers just back from the woods drew them into a pickup soccer game. Sam excelled at soccer. He easily controlled the ball, and he fed it to Frisco to make the goals.

They played long and hard. Each time he scored, Frisco grinned at Sam's celebrative slap on his burly shoulder.

The Dance

Days later, when Sam was telling Olympia about the soccer game, he said the physical contact and Frisco's grin had started a change in the relationship with his chief ranger.

She nodded. "Sometimes *appropriate* physical touch communicates in ways words can't."

"Now I have to start leaning on him about those shelters and cobwebs in the pavilion."

They were again atop the seawall. Below, a boat approaching the docks was delivering the last of the season's tourists.

"Talk about different personalities!" Sam declared. "Giselle and Henry are from different planets, yet they both responded to a bit of personal time."

"Plus a little gift for Henry."

"I just picked it out for him. He bought it. He's really been on board ever since."

"And Giselle?"

"She hasn't been finger-pointing, and she actually had her staff pump up the urgency of getting those levees repaired." He paused. "But she's still Giselle. I'll never hear her purr in a staff meeting. Something's still eating at her, and she still has those extremely sharp claws."

"But you're making progress. Keep at it."

He said he had a lot of issues to face and tough meetings ahead. Olympia said it came with the territory.

"I know, and I'm not complaining. I'm amazed at all the progress."

Olympia nodded. "It happens one by one, as people experience authentic appreciation from their leaders. Then they spread it to colleagues."

Sam smiled at the thought of Briana and Jackson chattering in the shelter.

The last boat of the season had docked and tourists were descending onto the shore. Sam thought how intensely satisfying it was that Spruce Isle hadn't flooded and that those visitors were heading for good times.

Olympia turned toward him, sunlight brightening her colorful bill. "Have you ever seen a puffin dance?"

What an unexpected question! Sam could hardly imagine her odd shape and orange feet rhythmically bouncing on the rocks. "No, I've never seen a puffin dance. I didn't know they did."

"We swim, and we dive, and we fly, and we kiss our

lifetime mates—and we dance!"

He could see she was enjoying his look of surprise. "We puffins know how to celebrate. After the storm was over, and dawn lit up the island, I saw the seawalls had held back the devastation. And I noticed those beautiful red streaks on the clouds. That's when I danced on the high, wet rocks."

Sam smiled. "I wish I'd seen you. Show me now."

She laughed. "Of course not!"

They watched as the last of the passengers disembarked.

Olympia said, "Sam, why do you think I told you I danced when the dawn came?"

He gave her a "tell-me" look.

The wise old bird said, "My dance was for you! There's a lot more to leadership than grim, get-it-done stuff. There's celebration! And it all starts with affirming the dignity and uniqueness of every person." Olympia playfully moved her feet. "A leader needs appreciation like anybody else. I celebrated for what you accomplished—and for who you are."

She lifted her wings, about to take flight. "So, Sam," she said, "I'll say it again: Everyone needs appreciation, not just for what they do, but for who they are."

. . . .

The end of the fable
(But not the book)

Leaders' Insights
from *Sync or Swim*

We sent our fable to leaders in various fields and asked for feedback. "I loved it," a trainer emailed. "It describes exactly what's going on in so many workplaces." A CEO said that as she interacts with leaders in other workplaces she hears similar stories.

You may have seen similarities from your own experiences. We invite you to scan these insights from readers and, in a sense, join the conversation. We selected comments we thought could be most relevant and helpful. Many were very personal, emphasizing the raw realities of leading teams or confessing to past failures related to what they saw in the fable.

Hopefully their comments will spark new insights and fruitful ideas for you.

"Sam's mistake was my mistake."

Over and over we heard that Sam's failed celebration was all too familiar. A respondent told us, recalling one of his own that fell flat, "I wish I'd known then what this story shows." Another said with a grin, "I loved it when Sam decided the way to capture the hearts and minds of employees was to throw a party. Sure it was! New supervisors feel they're like superheroes flying in."

A manager was amused at Sam's buoyant feeling of "bring it on" and warned of the trap of overconfidence. "We all feel sometimes we can rise to the challenge when others cannot." Another confessed, "For most of my career, I led my groups the way Sam started out. I would come to a new position filled with exuberance and confidence. I thought I had the magic recipe and that my can-do attitude and encouragement would bring everybody on board. I wish back then I'd had the fable's wisdom—that each individual needs to be appreciated and valued differently."

For some respondents, Sam's emotions after the failure and being mocked as the Mighty Motivator brought back raw memories. A manager told us, "Sometimes you feel like crawling into a hole. You work hard and think you've done a good thing, but the celebration comes off contrived. Criticism can be crushing. You fantasize like Sam did—I used to dream of escaping and working in a little flower shop."

Trust must precede celebratory events. "In my academic setting," a respondent told us, "I was impressed by a new leader's first spending time listening to groups all over campus. It was a significant time investment that paid off. We all want to make a great impression and start out strong. But we need to start out listening."

"I've seen every one of these characters."

An executive told us his one-time production chief was like Frisco the bear. "The man was six-foot-three, had poor people skills, and projected, 'I know what I'm doing.' But he didn't, and he wasn't interested in advice. He made a huge, costly mistake."

Frisco was mentioned many times as a familiar character. Said one respondent, "The bear didn't want help clearing trees because he valued self-sufficiency. I have this tendency myself and have family members firmly entrenched in it. With this mindset, independence supersedes interdependence, and people fail to communicate appreciation to others because they don't notice what others are doing."

One of Olympia's most-mentioned quotes was, "If you're going to be a leader, know your followers." One manager said after decades of leadership he was well familiar with all the characters in the fable. "To be frank, forty years ago I would have treated everyone the same way. I've learned to manage people differently and appreciate their differences."

Another leader said Olympia's know-your-followers advice made him seriously reflect on his business and personal life. "I have always been an influential leader, and I mainly focused on working on the quality of who I am, what I do, and what I offer. Though I've always taken people into consideration and tried to serve them, I haven't spent enough focused time on knowing my followers. That is, until now."

Yet another respondent said the know-your-followers quote summed up the entire fable. "The whole story resonated as to how important it is to know your employees and build that relationship and trust. Only then can you change the culture. You need to start one person at a time."

How? One respondent advised looking for clues and mentioned Jackson the beaver. "The engineer was so proud of his red pickup! Noticing what a guy like that highly values can give you big clues about what you can do to make *them* feel valued."

"It's not natural for me to be affirming."

Let's face it—for some of us it's not easy to keep looking for authentic ways to affirm people. One veteran manager admitted, "I come from a stoic German background where doing a good job is what's expected, not something to be praised. I've had to fight against that." Having recently completed her MBA, she said that studying the way positive expectations lift the bottom line changed her management style.

Plenty of research supports that. For instance, Shawn Achor's *The Happiness Advantage* quotes study after study on the ways positive psychology "fuels success and performance at work." Our respondent with the new MBA now sees in a fresh way how affirmation is crucial to effectiveness. "But," she says from experience, "not everyone believes that!"

"Build with Briana?"

We found it significant that many respondents recognized Briana as a type of employee who could spark positivity in a dysfunctional organization. "When changing a culture," said one manager, "it starts slowly by building trust, relationships, and finding that champion for change. In the story, I thought Briana represented that person. She was new, was enthusiastic despite others' negative attitudes, and with the changes found a reason to stay in the organization."

Not only young stars have potential to grow. Said one manager, "It takes time to understand the people around me, to figure out how to help each person understand the message I'm trying to get across. It takes me a while to figure out how to show each person I value them. I have to build an emotional bridge before we can get down to business together."

Often, though, there's little time to do that, and in today's fast-moving workplace, it takes determination to notice the clues. "In our industry," one leader told us, "change happens daily. We have multiple layers, and each person is different. When you're in charge of many employees, change, culture, and appreciation start with the top leader and trickles down to the frontline."

"Yes, I've wanted to dump the touchy-feely stuff."

"Boy," said a manager, "have I ever felt like Sam—not wanting to hold people's hands in a crisis! Sometimes we just have to suck it up and get down to business."

We repeatedly heard what we knew to be true—managers now feel terrific pressure. With resources limited or non-existent, they're weary of running out of solutions for tough challenges and can feel overwhelmed. Fear of losing their jobs fuels anxieties. They're pressured to do more with less and meet stretch goals. Some see the "soft stuff" as a distraction.

Yet the manager who identified with Sam confided, "I've learned my staff needs the hand-holding and recognition the most during the very rough times."

It's often hard to squeeze in "people time," but it's essential.

The manager also said, "My problem was I needed someone to hold *my* hand, but there wasn't anyone to do that!"

For everyone at every level, authentic appreciation and recognition are vital.

"The puffin's right— authentic appreciation spreads."

Ever wonder why in some organizations almost everyone radiates enthusiasm and goodwill? Leadership at the top, of course, sets the tone, but leaders can't do everything. Yet they can set in motion a ripple effect. One survey found peer-to-peer recognition is 36 percent more likely to have a positive impact on financial results than manager-only recognition.

Respondents strongly approved this from Olympia: "It happens one by one, as people experience authentic appreciation from their leaders. Then they spread it to their colleagues." One commented, "People not only need to connect with the boss, they need to connect with each other in friendship. Having friends at work is one of the great job 'satisfiers.' So long as they don't become a clique, it's a great motivator and healthy dimension of a work environment.

"Managers should recognize and foster those friendships."

"It's not profound—it's everyday simple."

Several managers resonated with Olympia's comment that sometimes all it takes is helping someone with a task. "Such wisdom in this simple statement," said one. "Sometimes we think it has to be big or profound, but it's just the everyday stuff that makes a big difference."

Another observed, "Olympia is so right—and tone of voice and body language often say more than words. When I need to talk to someone, I never ask the person to come see me. That can be intimidating, so I go to their cubicle. I'm six-foot six, and that can also be intimidating, so I sit down. Nonverbal signals are more important than we may realize."

Another leader agreed. "I appreciated Sam's willingness to go to each report and talk where they worked. That showed he was interested in what they did, how they did it, and what they needed to do it better."

Some very old wisdom may apply: "What you do every day is much more important than what you do once in awhile."

"Sam might have to fire Giselle."

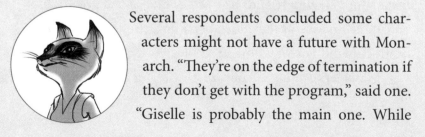

Several respondents concluded some characters might not have a future with Monarch. "They're on the edge of termination if they don't get with the program," said one. "Giselle is probably the main one. While

Sam and Giselle seem to have come to terms, I'm not sure how long that will last. The Giselles in my life haven't always come around—a supervisor who 'pollutes staff morale' and makes others fear her represents a deep problem not easily corrected. Sam had a good idea to get Tia's advice on how to approach Giselle, but eventually he'll need to have a very serious talk with her."

Another cautioned, "If this type of person doesn't come around after adequate attention, explanation, training, and encouragement, it's best they move on."

It wasn't just Giselle who raised concerns. One respondent commented, "Alana's power made me cringe." This respondent told us he once worked with a toxic colleague strongly positioned with the CEO and board "who had the ability to take down anyone—and he frequently used it. Good senior people were fired."

Those cautions matched another manager's counsel: "Don't forget the dark side!" He described causes for toxic environments including incompetent employees, avoidance of problems, and people with agendas at odds with management's. But his most serious caution was this: "Some people are actually evil. They lie, steal, and subtly undermine leadership and morale. They're toxic. They need to be moved toward the door as soon as legally possible." He added, "Don't give the impression that affirming each person according to their individuality will solve all your problems. That's very important!"

We heartily agree. In fact, his advice especially resonates with us because we have been deeply engaged interviewing people in toxic workplaces. We've become painfully aware of how many toxic leaders and toxic workplaces today are ruining people's lives. The result of the research is our recently released *Rising Above Your Toxic Workplace,* from the same publisher as *Sync or Swim.* In it, people who have lived through poisonous situations describe their struggles and personal solutions, and we include an extensive Survival Guide to provide help for those in unhealthy workplaces.

So we are quick to agree individual affirmations don't solve all problems. At the same time, research and experience show it's powerful. Several respondents picked the following as Olympia's key takeaway: "What's vital is communicating authentic appreciation. It's organizational oil."

"Find your Olympia."

Typical of comments about Olympia's advice was this: "Just about everything Olympia said was a valuable 'aha' insight. Her ideas were fresh, clear, and practical. Even her method of communicating with Sam is a good example for supervisors."

Among the principles deemed most important were these:

- Changing a culture requires a whole new way of communicating.
- Take time to listen to each person who reports to you. Watch for nonverbal signals.
- Keep your messages short and sweet, in languages they understand, with actions they value.
- Sarcasm is poison.
- When workers feel used and not valued, rewarding them backfires.
- Team members want to be valued for who they are, not just what they produce. They're persons, not replaceable parts.
- Become the Great Listener.

Absorbing Olympia's principles is key, yet as one respondent pointed out, at times we need a real-life Olympia. She went on to describe a mentor in her life as "wise and knowledgeable and could do the hard things. He was kind, understanding, grace-giving, and would offer wise counsel." How did that help her? She confided, "When you're beaten up, it's so helpful to have someone with objectivity say to you, 'This isn't about you personally. It's about a set of circumstances, emotions, and conditions, and something can be done about that.'"

We were also intrigued by another manager's comment: "Olympia seems like the Peter Drucker of the fable."

As you likely know, Drucker as "the father of modern

management" long ago jump-started the remarkable train of practical, informed workplace wisdom that eventually included authors such as Warren Bennis, Jim Collins, John Maxwell, and Stephen Covey. New research keeps reinforcing the validity of Drucker's philosophy that was based on his core, essential principle: that we are all made in the image of God.

That's why respect and appreciation are not frills on the agenda. They are vital to teamwork and effectiveness.

"What a great ending!"

Like Sam, some of our respondents in the thick of the battle have learned to give authentic appreciation, but that doesn't mean they receive it themselves. One told us, "I was especially moved by the ending. This is certainly something I would love to experience." Another said, "What a great ending! Sadly, many people don't understand how important celebration is. Too often there's little or none."

Celebration! Sometimes it's hard to come by. Sam still faces lots of stiff challenges, and so do most of us. But every time we listen, comprehend, and affirm, we sneak in celebration.

The puffin's dance—yes, puffins really do dance!—struck some respondents as representing the celebratory theme we should keep alive as we interact with coworkers who are made in God's image.

Questions for Reflection and Discussion

One of the best ways to remember information is to share with others what you are learning. Additionally, an effective way to deepen understanding of new concepts is to reflect on how they apply to your daily life and to hear others' perspectives on the same information. To help in this process, we've put together questions you can reflect on or use as a guide to discuss with others who have read the story of Sam and his colleagues.

- What challenges do you face in your workplace relationships? How might authentic appreciation help you deal with your most difficult personnel problems?

- Which of the characters in the story tended to annoy you the most? Why? How do you relate to individuals in your daily life who are like that character?

- Which of the characters did you most identify with? What qualities do you think you share with them? What in the story challenged you to think about behaviors, thoughts, or attitudes you may want to change?

- Do you find communicating appreciation natural, or do you find it hard? Are there tips in the story or managers' responses that might make it more "do-able" for you?

- Have you ever tried your best to show recognition to a group or individual and been rebuffed as Sam was? If so, how did you handle it?

- What, if anything, about Sam did you admire? What were characteristics about him that irritated or concerned you? In what ways did you see Sam grow over the course of events?

- Which of Olympia's statements are most helpful for you?

- Which piece of advice from Olympia do you think would be most difficult to implement in your current workplace? Why? What might help overcome these challenges?

- Are there any of Olympia's suggestions with which you disagree? Explain.

- Sam would have been justified to give up on Frisco, yet he didn't. What is the balance between too much patience and too little?

- When looking at the characters who work for Monarch Enterprises, what challenges do you think they would face in building an effective team?

- If you could pick three of Sam's colleagues to form a core group for a team you would manage, who would you pick and why?

- What issues do you think Sam should pay attention to and address in the next stage of working with his team?

The Fable's Core Principles

1

Not everyone feels appreciated in the same ways. "One size" *doesn't* fit all—that is why most employee recognition programs are ineffective. We each have our own preferred language of appreciation and specific actions that are meaningful to us.

2

We have identified five effective languages of appreciation common in the workplace:

Words of Affirmation. A simple verbal compliment or word of encouragement, expressed either orally or in writing.

Quality Time. Communicating value by giving your focused attention, or inviting the person to spend time with you and other colleagues.

Acts of Service. A simple act that can help make a colleague's day go better (e.g., working with them to ensure that a time-sensitive project is completed).

Tangible Gifts. A small gift that shows that you are getting to know what your coworker likes (e.g., bringing in a snack you know they enjoy).

Physical Touch. Spontaneous celebration of a positive result—a fist-bump when a project is completed, or a congratulatory handshake when a sale is closed.

3

Appreciation must be communicated in ways important to the recipient (not the sender). Most of us attempt to show appreciation in ways meaningful to *us.* Those with whom we work are often encouraged in different ways.

4

People want to feel valued by both their supervisors and *colleagues.* One mistake employee recognition programs make is to focus primarily on "top→down" relationships.

While employees want to know they are appreciated by their supervisors, individuals also want to know they are valued by their colleagues.

5

Appreciation must be viewed as authentic. When recipients doubt the genuineness of recognition—when they consider appreciation *inauthentic*—apathy, cynicism, and mistrust grow. Authenticity is at the heart of healthy workplace relationships.

For a more thorough discussion and explanation of the importance of appreciation in the workplace and how to help those with whom you work truly *feel* appreciated, see the following resources.

Resources

- 5 *Languages of Appreciation in the Workplace: Empowering Workplaces by Encouraging Employees*, by Dr. Gary Chapman and Dr. Paul White (Northfield Publishing, 2011).

- The *Motivating by Appreciation* Inventory. An online assessment that identifies the preferred language and actions of appreciation valued by the respondent.

- *Appreciation at Work* implementation kit. A tool to help leaders and work groups apply the concepts of authentic appreciation in the workplace. Includes DVDs, a facilitator's guide, and handouts.

- *AppreciationatWork.com*. Provides free articles, videos, and other resources to learn how to communicate appreciation in the workplace.

- *Sync or Swim* webpage. Find additional resources directly related to the *Sync or Swim* fable and characters. *www.appreciationatwork.com/syncorswim*

- *Rising Above a Toxic Workplace: Taking Care of Yourself in an Unhealthy Environment* by Dr. Gary Chapman, Dr. Paul White, and Harold Myra (Northfield Publishing, 2014).

- *Toxic workplaces information.* Find out how toxic your workplace is and identify the most troubling areas to address. Discover resources that will help improve the critical areas identified. *www.appreciationatwork.com/toxicworkplaces*

* Note: Each of these resources can be found at or accessed through www.appreciationatwork.com.

Acknowledgments

M any minds and hands helped create this little book. Betsey Newenhuyse added her creative editing and fresh ideas, John Hinkley hacked through the underbrush of publishing challenges, and Zack Williamson connected the story with readers and came up with the title. Seasoned leaders from a wide range of organizations provided lively, practical responses. Our thanks to Beth Allison, Jo Lynn Bright, Judy Bryson, Maria Elena Duron, George and Marjean Fooshee, Peter Hart, Lori Hartline, Tim Hepner, Les Hirst, John LaRue, Cathie Leimbach, Dana McArthur, Dean Merrill, Caroline Rochon, Roy Saunderson, Kari Schauss, Eric Schmidt, Keith Stonehocker, and David Tippett.

About the Authors

GARY CHAPMAN, one of America's most popular relationship experts, is author of the #1 *New York Times* bestseller *The 5 Love Languages* and numerous other popular books. He travels the world presenting seminars. Find out more at 5lovelanguages.com.

PAUL WHITE is a psychologist, author, and speaker who helps businesses make "work relationships work." He has consulted with a wide variety of organizations including Microsoft, DirecTV, the Million Dollar Round Table, Princeton University, and many more. He and Gary Chapman coauthored *The 5 Languages of Appreciation in the Workplace*.

HAROLD MYRA has written more than two dozen fiction and nonfiction books, including *The Leadership Secrets of Billy Graham*. During his thirty-two years as CEO of a magazine publishing company, the organization grew from one magazine to thirteen while establishing a thriving Internet site.

visit

---

appreciationatwork.com

for free tools and resources that
will help you in the workplace.

More Resources on Workplace Dynamics

Many today are experiencing the reality of bullying bosses, poisonous people, and soul-crushing cultures on a daily basis. Insightfully illustrating from real-life stories, *Rising Above a Toxic Workplace* delivers practical hope and guidance for those who find themselves in an unhealthy work environment.

978-0-8024-0972-0 | also available as an eBook

From psychologist and consultant Dr. Paul White comes *The Vibrant Workplace*, a field guide for rooting out negativity and cultivating trust in every level of your organization. Readers will learn how organizational culture works, how to facilitate systemic change over time, and why appreciation is the key to healthy teams.

978-0-8024-1503-5 | also available as an eBook

NORTHFIELD
PUBLISHING

Appreciation at Work™ Implementation Kit

Appreciation at Work™ Online Training Course

Become a certified facilitator and help others discover how to empower organizations by encouraging people.

IDEAL FOR:

- Human Resource professional or internal corporate trainer
- Business or organizational coach, consultant, or trainer
- Supervisor or Team Leader

FOR MORE INFORMATION ABOUT TRAINING RESOURCES, VISIT **appreciationatwork.com/train**.

Appreciation at Work

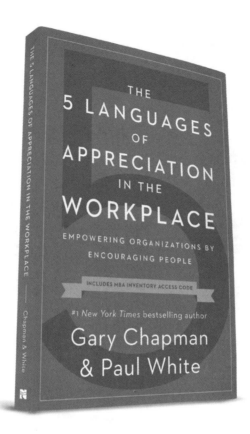

DR. PAUL WHITE
"MAKING WORK RELATIONSHIPS WORK."

Dr. Paul White is available for speaking and training for businesses, organizations, and associations.

Please visit:
drpaulwhite.com
to see video clips, potential topics, training resources, and other details of how Dr. White can serve your organization.

The 5 Languages of Appreciation
WHERE YOU WORK.

THE MOTIVATING BY APPRECIATION INVENTORY
**Discover which language of appreciation "hits the mark"
to make you feel valued at work!**

- The Basic version of the MBA Inventory is a brief / direct version applicable to virtually all work settings.

- The MBAI Expanded version provides an in-depth report comparing your results with the general workforce population (text and graphic charts), identifying the single most important act of appreciation to you, and identifies the actions not desired in each language of appreciation.

GENERAL WORK SETTING VERSION

 Government

 Military

 Long Distance

 Ministry / Not For Profit

 Medical

 School

We feel passionate about helping people wherever they work. As a result of working together with a variety of industries, we have developed versions of the MBA Inventory that address the unique characteristics and relational dynamics for each of the above work settings.

**For more information about training resources,
visit appreciationatwork.com/assess.**

STAY CONNECTED
and take the next step . . .

ONLINE

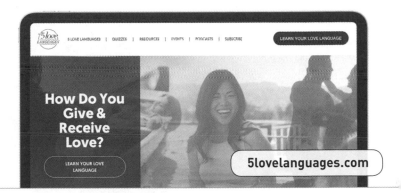

How Do You Give & Receive Love?

LEARN YOUR LOVE LANGUAGE

5lovelanguages.com

APP

LOVE NUDGE™ FOR COUPLES IS LIKE A FITNESS APP FOR RELATIONSHIPS

A playful engaging tool that helps couples experience love more deeply

SOCIAL

- 📘 /5lovelanguages
- 📷 /@5lovelanguages
- 🐦 /drgarychapman
- 𝑣 /drgarychapman
- ▶ /user/drgarychapman